Book Title

Stay Schemin

Authored by Emmanuel Philippe

Preface

This book is just to teach curious minds of the basic frauds that is out there so no one falls victim. I've been a victim of many fraud/scams which is how I ended up being involved in scamming, I'm not going to lie I'm very petty - my slogan in my teenage years was "I don't get mad, I get even." Let's face it nobody likes being a victim, so I myself joined the winning team and that's when my life took a turn for the worst. I was getting arrested left and right, I became a target in my neighborhood because broke dudes would always try to rob me since they thought they had an idea of what my income was, based on the cars I was driving and the jewelry I had.

Even the females tried their angles with me, everybody was after one thing and that was free easy money and shopping sprees. I started driving around with pistols and AR-15s to protect myself, which is how I caught my federal time. I was so paranoid and living on the edge, it's a blessing I have this opportunity to write this book. In prison once people find out I know about fraud, they start latching onto me in hopes I teach them the craft because they're tired of selling drugs or doing home invasions etc. People constantly asking is what sparked the idea that I should write a book on this, I am not encouraging anybody to go out and commit any crimes.

Trust me you will pay the price if you do, every game from drugs to fraud is a losing game. There's too many cameras, informants, under covers, and technology period to think you can be evasive and win. This book is an educational tool to help business owners, and the average Joe protect their self and their assets.

Stay tuned for part Two of this book where I

will break down the different types of fraud, such as income tax fraud, real estate fraud, and more.

If you are an author seeking publication or interested in selling your manuscript across various genres, please feel free to reach out to me via email at mannyphil@traphousepublishing.com. Kindly include three chapters from your manuscript, along with the book title, subtitle, and descriptions.

For further updates and information, you can also find me on the following social media platforms:

- Instagram: Red_Dotceo

- Facebook: Manny Phil

- TikTok: James_Stpatric

- Snapchat: Red_Dot9

I look forward to hearing from you and exploring the potential of your literary work.

TABLE OF CONTENT

CHAPTER ONE :

LINGO

101's - Credit Cards without security. Most prepaid/gift cards are considered 101.

201's - Credit Cards with security, you must dip inside POS terminal to process purchases.

Bin Number - First (six) digit of any credit card number, those numbers identify the issuing bank, and the relevant network on which the card operate.

Touch Down - TD Bank

Chevy - Chase

Itty or Litty - City Bank

B.O.A - Bank of America

Fargo - Wells Fargo Bank

Tander - Santander Bank Cap - Capital one Bank

Amex - American Express

Disco - Discover Bank

Gifty - Gift Cards

Voodoo Piece - A credit card that never declines, those are usually business cards or wealthy people cards.

Inny - A plug/insider who works at a any store that sells valuables, and let scammers buy unlimited things for a fee

O.T - Out of town or out of state

On the Road - outside scamming

L's, Face, and I's - pronounced (eyes), all three means drivers license or I.D.

Profiles - A persons identity information, which includes D.O.B, address, social security number, etc..O - Money orders Nikes - checks Bounty - Counterfeit moneyWesty - Western Union

Renty - Rental Car

P.O.S - Point of sale machine that accept all credit card/debit payment for in store purchases.

M.S.R - Magnetic strip reader that's used to add bank information on fraudulent credit cards.

M.I.C.R - Magnetic ink character reader that captures consumers account #, routing #, and check number to cash or validate checks.

P.E.D - Pin Entry Device is a skimmer device scammers place over a real retail P.O.S machine to steal debit/credit card info and PIN number.

Lit Food - Valid account numbers that's not going to decline.

V.P.N - Virtual Private Network that hides your computer IP address, and let you browse the dark web privately. Which makes it harder for law enforcement to trace their steps.

Burn Last 4 - Certain stores ask for the last 4 of the card number to complete the purchase. When a scammer run out of cards/material, they usually recycle old cards by leaving the first 12 numbers and burn the last 4 digits by placing a lighter under it, and moving it back and forth slowly until the numbers embossed number disappears.

Batch Typically refers to bulk credit card orders.
Dumps - Stolen credit card numbers that are for sale.
Cvv - Is a 3 digit security number on the back of a credit card, located next to the signature strip.
Cash out Man - A person who buys merchandise from scammers in bulk at discount rates, to resell at higher value.

Head - A person that is used as a pawn. They often open accounts in their names for scammers and cash checks for them, or finance phones out of stores, etc.

Free up Money - Funds that becomes available after you deposit a check on the account, it's usually around $2-$300.

Drop - A certain time frame scammers drop checks into an account either through mobile banking or physical ATM. This process is done during bank closing hours around 6-9pm, then they wait a few hours for the funds to clear usually 3-7 AM.

Hot Spot or Burned Down - Locations that are risky for scammers due to high fraud activity.

Mobile Dump - Depositing checks in bank account, using the banking app.

Clip - credit card or check is no longer valid, it's been closed or red flagged.

Red Flagged - When banks freeze an account for suspicious/fraudulent activities.

CHAPTER 2:

Apps and Website

Below are some apps and websites that most scammers use to either defraud or communicate with Allies or their victims.

Blockchain - A cryptocurrency wallet that is used to purchase or sell crypto. Cryptocurrency such a bitcoin are commonly used by scammers on the dark web to make purchases.

Skout - An app used to locate every store in any state and gives GPS directions. Scammers use this app to save time on finding stores when they are on unfamiliar territory (O.T).

ICQ - A chat room app used by scammers to advertise and sell profiles, Equipments, and banking information.

P.O.S apps/devices - Either your phone or Portable POS devices can be used to scam credit cards.

Cash App - An app that lets any user wire funds from their credit card at $0 cost instantly. Western Union App - International money wire transfers for a fee.

Uber App - Fancy taxi app

Telegram - Another encrypted scammer chat room.

Signal - Another chat room that saves no conversations. Trust App - Cryptocurrency wallet like blockchain.

Below are some active websites scammers use to buy Dumps, profiles, bank account log ins, etc. Realandrare.cc Bankcmat.cc Vclub.cc Benumb.cc Crdpro.cc savastan0.cc approved.tw limbo.cards Briansclub.cm

CHAPTER THREE:

Fraud Equipments

Fraud Equipments are surprisingly cheap and very easy to purchase. All the main components needed by scammers to commit fraud cost a measly $500. All the Equipments are legally sold on Amazon.com, eBay.com, brandh.com, digital ID, and Ding Word Ink. Below is a list of the most common used fraud Equipments.

Embosser 72 characters - A machine that is used to print the credit card holders name, card number and expiration date on the physical card.

MSR 605x USB card Reader Writer - A rectangle black brick that's used to add track 1, track 2, and 3 on credit magnetic strips before using them for purchases.

Hot foil stamping machine 10x13cm pvc - This is usually called a tipper in the fraud field, it's used to make the credit cards look more professionally done by stamping it with the foil machine.

Versacheck HP DeskJet 3755 check printer - This order includes laser ink printer, cartridges, software and blank check stock.

X6 BT Bluetooth card reader - Commonly known as black box in the streets, scammers give this machine to people who work at retail/restaurants who will swipe you card discretely and steal your card info.

P.O.S portable terminal - Used as a tool to steal funds from merchant accounts and random victim credit cards.

Ambir nScan 690Gt Card Scanner - A machine that's used in the counterfeit I.D trade.

Bodno Magicard 300 Dual sided ID card printer -The complete package along with ID software. Lap Top computer

Websites that sells these Equipments: eBay.com

Amazon.com

Bandh.com

Digital ID

Ding word ink

Chapter Four :

Purpose of the App

Blockchain is a digital wallet for virtual currency. When the app first came out it didn't have a lot of security feature, all a person need was an email and password. Due to Cryptocurrency being used in the underworld to commit crimes, alot of stricter guidelines have been added. To use this app now or even coinbase.com you must have government issued I.D or passport to create an account.

Blockchain allows its users to select from a wide variety of different cryptos, either for buying and selling or to make purchases. Once an account is created blockchain will provide you with a private key and public key, those numbers are what people will use to process payments.

Those numbers can be copied and pasted , there's also a QR code that can be scanned to save time.

Crypto keys is a unique string of numbers and letters of 26-35 characters in length that shows where a Bitcoin payment has been sent to and from. It looks something like this 5Kb8kLf9zgWQnogidDA76MzPL6TsZZY36hW XMssSzNydYXYB9KF. When scammers use websites like Briansclub.cm or any website to buy stolen information, this is how payments are processed.

Skout is a app all scammers use to locate every major store all over the U.S. The app give its users gps directions to the store exact location, and it keeps a log of stores that they already went too so they don't make the same mistake of going to the same store twice. Scammers find this app very helpful because when traveling to another state using google to locate store can be very hectic.

For example a person searching for a Walmart store using google - google might pin point a store all the way across town, when there might be 2 to 3 Walmart stores minutes away from each other near your exact location.

ICQ/Telegram are both similar but not the same. ICQ used to be a safe haven chatroom for all scammers just like the Crypto wallets security have changed so have ICQ. A lot of scammers migrated from ICQ to telegram where they sell profiles, cards, and other things that's part of the underworld trade. Both apps are encrypted, anybody can go on the app and play with the search engine to find what they are looking for.

Example to find scammers on ICQ/Telegram a user can type in anything from dumps, gift cards, cvv, bins, profiles, or any fraud keyword one can think of. Once a user searches for something many options will pop up, once an option is selected you can communicate with those users.

Cash app & Square: Both of these apps are tools scammers use for wire frauds, there are plenty other ways wire fraud is done which will be in Part 2 of stay schemin. Cash app allows its users to wire funds either from their debit/credit card or bank account straight to another cash app using a unique username which only belongs to them.

The square app is a little different, because it's an actual software that turns your phone or tablet into a portable POS system that accepts debit/credit card payments. The square POS is available online or any office supply stores.

The will ask for a bunch or personal information, which is why scammers keep a bunch of profiles and active prepaid/bank card on hand. Users need to enter name, email, date of birth, EIN number if the user don't have their EIN entering their social security number will satisfy the criteria. Lastly users will select which field their business is in then enter their banking information to be able to accept payments.

Scammers go online and buy stolen card information and create false invoices then charge them to people's credit card either by swiping it through the POS card reader, or by entering it manually. If approved it will indicate so and the signature pad on the receipt will pop up for a John Hancock, scammers can process the payments once it's been cleared by Square out of the merchant account to the banking account.

CHAPTER FIVE :

EQUIPMENT USE

The Embosser is what scammers use to put a name, expiration date, and 16digit number on the card. The Embosser has 4 key components. #1 is the spinning wheel on top of the machine with 72 characters that's also called a character disk, that includes letters, numbers, and symbols. #2 is the lever on the right side of the machine which is called the coding handle. #3 will be the small knob in front of the machine that has a 1/7 and 1/10 indication mark and the proper name for that is character interval knob. 1/7 inch is only for large characters such as for the 16digit card number, 1/10 inch is for small characters such as the card holders name on the bottom of the card. #4 is the metal sliding tray that holds the credit card in play while it's being embossed, the tray is labeled with (two) sets of numbers one set of numbers going horizontal and the other going vertically.

Those numbers on the credit card tray play a major role, because it let the user know what position the credit card is in. There are (three) positions. Position #1 starts at #7 on the vertical line, the horizontal line stays on position 0-1 with the tray slid all the way to the left. This
position is used to emboss the card 16 digit number, the character interval stays on 1/7 position. Credit card numbers are always a bigger font then the name and expiration date.

The character wheel on top of the Embosser can turn in either direction, to emboss a character the lever on the right side must be pulled all the way to emboss the characters on the card. For space the lever is not pulled but slightly tapped.

The second position on the Embosser is lining up the credit card tray on #9 vertically, the lever on the right is tapped to space the tray slot all the way to #15 vertically. Alignment 9-15 is usually where the credit card expiration date goes, with the interval knob on 1/10 mark.

Third position is the final one, which is where the name goes on the credit card. The interval knob stays in 1/10 mark, the card tray is pushed all the way up vertically to the last number, and the card tray slid all the way to the left on the 0 mark to start embossing a name.

The MSR is a rectangular black card reader, it comes with a software disk and USB cable to hook up to a lap top. The MSR street name is read and writer, the read and writer has 3 different color light indicators that have different meanings - those colors are red, yellow, and green.

When the reader and writer is connected/ready for use the light indicator will be green, the green light is also indication that the card information on track 1, 2, and 3 have been successfully written and cloned. Yellow light is indication that the MSR is on stand by mode waiting for a card to be swiped for reading or writing information on that card.

Once a card is swiped the MSR light indicator can either turn green or red, red means something went wrong with the process.

Either the magnetic strip on the card is ruined or the MSR could be dusty. Once an MSR is successfully hooked up and the disk files are opened a small screen will pop up with track 1-3. On the right hand side there's selections for card type, data type, along with the read, write, copy, delete buttons etc.

Magnetic strips are logically divided into tracks or records that is used for storing the data required during financial transaction. Tracks are placed in a sequential order where track 1 is followed by track 2 and 3. The reading of the data also follows the same order.

Tracks 1 and 2 are mostly used to store crucial data, track 3 is used for storing optional data. Depending on the banks choice, they can store financial details on either tracks. Both these tracks follow specific format for storing the data.

Track 1 format: SS: Start sentinel (%) FC: Format code PAN: Primary Account Number FS: Field separator (^) CN: Card holders name (up to 26 characters long) ED: Expiration date (in the form, YY/MM)

SC: Service code

DD: Discretionary date (may include the card verification value [Cvv]/code, the pin verification value and the pin verification key indicator)

ES: End sentinel

LRC: Longitudinal redundancy check Track 2 Format:

SS: Start sentin

PAN: Primary account number

FS: (up to 19 digits long) FS: Field separator (=)

CN: Card Holders name (up to 26 characters long)

ED:Expiration date (in the form of, YY/MM)

SC: Service code

DD: Discretionary data

ES: End sentinel (?)

LRC: Longitudinal redundancy check

Here's an example of what a typical track dumps looks like.

Track1:B4096654104697113^John/Doe^080610127359 00521000000

Track 2:361344212572004=0512052335136; John/Doe

Both track 1 and 2 store information in blocks where each block represents specific value, each having a storage limit and separated by delimiters. Let's use **Track 1 as an example**.

Consider no value for SS and FC, the first seventeen characters represent the bank account number (B4096654104697113) followed by the field separator (^) and account holders name (John Doe). The next (Four) characters represent the card expiration date in YY/MM format (12/29). The next few numbers that follows are the cards service code (1012735900) and the identification number (521). The remaining digits are the fillers for the remaining byte.

Track 1 alone contains enough information to be converted into track 2. There are also plenty online tools that help scammers do this conversion with ease. Trackgenerator.Net is one such online service, most card websites sell track 2 data. But track 1 alone is sufficient enough to use a clone card for purchases, scammers can leave track 2 and 3 blank.

After the credit card has been read/written and embossed, the hot foil tipper comes into play. The tipper comes with 3 different color ribbons - green, red, and gold. Once the tipper is plugged in to a power outlet and turned on, it will began to heat up. Like the Embosser the tipper also have a metal tray that holds the credit card in place, there's a spot above the tray where the ribbon go. Lastly there's a lever on the side of the tipper and when pulled, the pressure plate that have the ribbons on it closes and it add professional holographic designs and colors to the card.

CHAPTER 6:

Credit/Debit Cards 1 on 1

Credits cards are a relatively recent development. The VISA Company, for example, traces its history back to 1958 when the Bank of America began its Bank Americard program. In the mid-

1960s, the Bank of America began to license banks in the United States the rights to issue its special Bank Americards. In 1977 the name Visa was adopted internationally to cover all these cards. VISA became the first credit card to be recognized worldwide.

The banks and companies that sponsor credit cards profit in three ways. Primarily they make money from the interest payments charged on the unpaid balance, but they also can make money by charging an annual fee for the use of the card.

The income from this fee, which is typically only $50 or $75 per customer per year, can be substantial considering that the larger companies have tens of millions of customers. In addition, the sponsors make money by charging merchants a small percentage of income for the service of the card.

This arrangement is acceptable to the merchants because they can let their customers pay by credit card instead of requiring cash. The merchant makes arrangements to participate in a credit card program with a merchant bank, which in turn works with a card-issuing bank. The merchant bank determines what percentage of the total purchase value has to be paid by the merchant to the card-issuing bank.

The amount varies depending on the volume and type of business, but in general it is between 1-2%. A percentage of that amount is kept by the merchant bank as a transaction-processing fee.

For companies like American Express which sponsor cards, the processing fee may be significantly higher. Furthermore, sponsors may generate income by leasing credit card verification equipment to merchants (especially if the merchants can not afford to purchase the equipment themselves.) Finally, sponsors may profit by charging service fees for late payments.

Design

Credit cards are designed with complex security features to prevent the possibility of fraud. These features involve the card's account number, its signature panel, and its magnetic stripe.

The card's unique account number is the key piece of information needed to conduct a financial transaction and must be carefully protected. To prevent someone from using a wrong account number, or from making up a phony number, companies rely on the laws of statistics for protection.

By using long account numbers they make it unlikely that a number can be faked.

For example, the Visa card has 13 digits, American Express has 15, Diners Club 14, and MasterCard has 20. Mathematically, nine digits would provide one billion unique account numbers (000000000, 000000001, 0000000002, and so forth up to 999999999) which would be enough for all the customers of a given company.

(The largest companies, Visa and MasterCard, only have about 65 million customers.) If only 65 million numbers are assigned out of a possible 10 trillion possibilities, it is unlikely that anyone will be able to mistakenly use another account number. If an incorrect account number is mistakenly entered by a store clerk, it will almost certainly not be accepted. This statistical security gives companies confidence that someone is not making up a number when conducting business over the phone. Of course, this security measure does not help if someone obtains a real number and uses it fraudulently.

Another security design feature involves the signature panel on the back of the card. The signature is intended to document the owner's handwriting so a forged signature on a receipt can be detected. To prevent criminals from erasing the back panel of a stolen card and putting on their own signature, the panel is printed with a fingerprint design that is difficult to duplicate and that will come off when the original signature is erased. If the signature is erased, this design will disappear too leaving a white spot, which instantly indicates the card has been tampered with. Some card manufacturers imprint the word VOID beneath this panel, which is revealed upon erasure.

The magnetic stripe on the back of the card is a third security feature. The stripe is an area coated with particles of iron oxide that can be encoded with binary information, which identifies the card as authentic. It is difficult to determine exactly what information is coded on the strip because for security reasons companies do not wish to discuss this.

However, it is likely that the card's expiration date is one fact recorded on the strip because automatic teller machines (ATMs) will retain cards that have expired. It is unlikely that information like credit limit, address, phone number, employer, is recorded on the stripe because banks do not reissue cards when this type of information changes.

Finally, some cards feature special features that make them hard to duplicate, such as complicated holograms.

"Bank Identification Number," or BIN code, refers to the initial sequence of four to six numbers that appears on a credit card. The number is used to identify the card's issuing bank or other financial institution.
The BIN number ties an issuer to all the cards it issues, and to all the transactions on those cards.

At the top of this page, you can use our BIN number lookup tool and use the credit card identifier system to determine the issuing bank of (almost) any payment card.

In the rest of this post, we'll take a closer look at these bank id numbers, what they mean, and how they may change in the future.

What Is a Bank Identification Number?

First, lets answer: what is a BIN? Like most industries, the payments sector is littered with its own slate of undecipherable acronyms and confusing argot.

The BIN is a perfect example. What is it? How does it differ from an IIN? And what do all those numbers mean, anyway?

The BIN (or bank identification code) is a numbering convention developed to identify which particular institution issued a given credit card or other bank card, and what type of institution it is. It's essentially the bank's calling card; each card-issuing bank has a unique BIN.

To start, let's look at the full set of numbers on the front of a typical bank card. This numbering system applies to credit/charge cards, debit cards, prepaid cards, and certain electronic benefit cards. For the purposes of this article, we lump them all together under the blanket term "payment card."

The first six digits are traditionally called the Bank Identification Number. It's becoming more common, however, to use the term Issuer Identification Number, or IIN. This reflects an increasing number of non-bank institutions who opt into the BIN network. However, the terms IIN and BIN can be used more or less interchangeably.

In either case, the number can vary between four and six digits, depending on the specific institution that issued the card. While using the first six numbers is the most common, it isn't mandatory, and even that may change soon, as we'll discuss later.

The Major Industry Identifier

The first digit of the card number is the Major Industry Identifier, or MII, and it possesses a certain significance on its own. The MII identifies the category or type of institution which issued the card. Visa- and MasterCard-branded cards, for example, are primarily issued by banks, and so they are classified as financial payment cards. Diner's Club and American Express are considered travel and entertainment cards, as this was their primary function at the time they debuted.

This chart spells out the MII codes by category: MII Digit Value Issuer Category0 ISO/TC 68 Assignment

1. Airline cards

2. Airlines cards (and other future industry assignments)

3. Travel and Entertainment Cards

4. Banking and Financial Cards

5. Banking and Financial Cards

6. Merchandising and Financial Cards

7. Gas Cards, Other Future Industry Assignments

8. Healthcare Cards, Telecommunications, Other Future Industry Assignments

9. For Use by National

Standards Bodies

To recap, when looking at the full bank card number, the first digit identifies the card issuer's industry, while the first six digits collectively identify the specific institution which issued the card. The remainder of the 16 (or 15, in some cases) digits make up the cardholders account number, including one or more check digits, also called a "checksum." A checksum represents the sum of a formula that helps determine if the credit card number is actually valid.

With the numbering combinations available, it is possible for each issuer to have about a trillion different account numbers for their cardholders.

How Bank Identification Numbers Help

The BIN/IIN provides merchants with a lot of other information besides just the issuing entity. For example, when cardholders enter card details for an online transaction, just those first few digits tell the retailer:

The name, address, and phone number of the bank funds will be transferred from The card brand (Visa, Mastercard, American Express, etc.)

What type of card it is (debit, credit, prepaid, etc.)

What level the card is (black, platinum, business)

Whether the issuer is in the same country as the device used in the transaction Whether the address provided by the cardholder matches the one on file

Finally, the BIN/IIN allows merchants to accept multiple forms of payment and speed up the overall processing.

Here are a few examples of the BIN format for the most widely-used card brands in the US:

Visa: 4*****

American Express (AMEX): 34*or 37****

Diner's Club: 36****

MasterCard: 51**** or 55****

Discover Card: 6011, 622126-622925, 644-649, 65.

As was previously mentioned 101 credit cards are

credit cards without the EMV security chip, 101 cards are basically extinct due to financial institutions trying to put a stop on fraudulent activities. Gift cards are most likely the only form of 101 cards left out there, the replacement for 101 cards is the 201s. The 201 card has a security EMV chip on it, there's 2 different kind of 201 cards.

The first kind is called a one dip, which means you dip the credit card inside the POS machine on the corner where the chip is located, the POS machine will read the chip and approve the purchase. The second 201 type is called a 3dip, a 1dip card is more expansive then the 3dip. The only difference is with the one dip after one attempt the POS machine will give an error message and demand the card be swiped, while a 3dip card you have to try 3 different times before the card can be swiped. The EMV chips on the cards are not real chips, and in rare cases if they are real - they will most likely be damaged so the POS machine can't read it.

Besides the BIN number, the most important number

on a credit card is the last 4 digits.

Those four digits normally show up on your receipt after a purchase, it is illegal for merchants to list anything more then those four numbers. Sometimes the store clerk behind the register msg ask for the last four of the card number so transaction may go through. Since the last four is crucial when it comes to purchases, instead of wasting time embossing a whole new card and throwing the old ones away scammers have a trick called burning the last four.

To burn the last four off a credit card, all that's needed is a lighter. They Place the flame of the lighter under the back side of the card, being careful not to damage the magnetic strip. They slowly move the lighter back and forth at a safe distance so it don't burn a hole through the plastic, the key is to heat the card up to the point where the embossed numbers start stretching and flattening. Next they put the card back in the Embosser and emboss the new 4 digit of the new dump they've just purchased.

When a scammer purchase credit card dumps from a website, it comes with the victims name, date of birth, address, and phone number, the victims social security number is not needed. The social is only need to check what is in the card holders savings, not the checking account available credit. To check the available balance on a bank card, scammers only need the 16 digit card number and zip code. What makes it so easy is they don't even have to talk to a real customer service agent, all of that is done with the voice automated system when they call.

Every scammer have a fake I.D in their possession, each card or check they create bears the same name that's on their I.D. When purchasing something on a credit transaction you must provide I.D and the name must match the name on the credit card, for debit purchase no I.D is needed. Another way around the I.D thing is using a phone for payment such as Apple Pay, google pay, paypal etc.

Scammers involved in bigger operations have the

means and tools to get any debit cards PIN number.

One of those tools is a skimmer device. Card skimming theft can affect anyone who uses their credit or debit cards at ATMs, gas stations, restaurants or retail stores. A skimmer is a device installed on card readers that collects card numbers.

Thieves will later recover and use this information to make fraudulent purchases. Skimmers can usually be spotted by doing quick visual or physical inspections before swiping or inserting a card.

Skimmers are most often found at ATMs and gas stations, but it's possible for retail stores or restaurants to be involved in a skimming scam as well. Sometimes a tiny camera is planted to record cardholders entering a PIN number into an ATM.

PIN numbers can also be stolen via fake keypads placed over a real ATM keypad. Skimmers and related technology can be hard to spot because thieves will attempt to make their devices blend in or match the style of the card readers.

Although skimmers can be hard to spot, it's possible to identify a skimming device by doing a visual and physical inspection.

Before using an ATM or gas pump, check for alignment issues between the card reader and the panel underneath it. Skimmers are often placed on top of the actual card reader making it stick out at an odd angle or cover arrows in a panel. Compare the card reader to others at a neighboring ATM or gas pump and look out for any differences.

Gas pumps should have a security tape or sticker over the cabinet panel. If the tape looks ripped or broken, avoid using the card reader because a thief may have tampered with it. Try looking inside the card reader to see if anything is already inserted—if there is, it may be a thin plastic circuit board that can steal card information.

A physical inspection of a card reader and keypad can often reveal fraudulent devices. Feel around the reader and try to wiggle it to see if it can easily come out of place.

The FTC has a photo example of a card skimming device on their website.

Authentic card readers are robustly manufactured, meaning if any part of the card reader can easily move around, then it's probably been installed illegally by a thief. If the buttons on an ATM's keypad are too hard to push, don't use that ATM and try another one.

Other Ways Cards Can Be Skimmed

It's much more difficult for a thief to install a card skimmer on a point-of-sale (POS) system at a retail store, but it can happen. Make sure the card reader looks as it should. If a restaurant is involved in a scam, there may be no way to know because cards are often handed to the server who can then swipe the card through a skimmer before giving it back to the customer.

How To Avoid Card Skimmers

Stay vigilant when using a credit card to pay for gas or when withdrawing cash at an ATM. If any part of a gas pump's card reader looks suspicious, pay for gas inside with the cashier and let them know there may be a skimmer installed at the pump.

Try to only use official bank ATMs instead of non bank ATMs that are often found inside convenience stores or bars. Cover fingers with the other hand while entering a pin to block potential cameras. Don't ever give a card to a credit card cleaner who claims he or she can clean the magnetic stripe or chip on a card to make it easier to read. These are often scams designed to steal credit card information.

Credit card skimming is a very lucrative scheme, with just 10-20 card pin information a scammer can get rich overnight. Every bank gives card holders an ATM limit of at least $1,000 a day, with an option to call up the bank and raise the ATM withdrawal limit in case of urgency/emergency. So that's an easy $10k-$20k a day or $70-140k a week - do the math.

You are wrong if you think hacking and skimming is the only way of scamming an individual!

There are many ways one can get trapped in fraudulent activities. Here are some of the examples;

1. Skimming

In this type of scam, your credit card details are stolen with the help of a device called a skimmer. When your card gets swiped through a skimmer, it stores all the data from your card. This information can then be duplicated on another card.

Thus, scammers use your credit card information to make monetary transactions. So, the next time you use credit cards, ensure you do not swipe through any machine that looks suspicious. You can also use chip-based credit cards; these are much more secure than those with a magnetic strip.

2. Dumpster Diving

Quite often, people casually discard bills or documents which contain their credit card details.

Anyone can collect them to retrieve their bank details and use them for scamming. This process is known as dumpster diving.

Hackers can use such documents with sensitive information for malpractices.

Therefore, the next time you have any such documents to discard, either shred them or scratch those details. Following certain precautionary steps can prevent you from getting trapped in such types of credit card scams in India.

3. Phishing

Phishing involves persuasion. Suppose you receive an email that looks convincing as it is from a well-known bank or financial organization. Your general reaction would be to click and check what it is about. Once you click on the link, it will redirect to a strange website where you are asked to put your personal information.

Most people fall into these traps. You must always remember banks do not generally send emails requesting your details. If you ever receive any such email or SMS, make sure to inform your credit card issuer so that you do not get into the trap. In addition, you must be very observant while replying to any such email or SMS.

4. Keystroke Capturing

Hackers mostly use keystroke logging through certain software to find your credit card details. This can happen if you click on a link redirecting you to download malware, and you unknowingly do that.

If any such software gets installed in your system, it will record every key that you press. Hence your ids and passwords are recorded as well.

To avoid any such situation, make sure not to click on any suspicious links. You can also use a virtual keyboard while feeding personal information like passwords and id details. Lastly, you must have reliable antivirus software to protect your system.

5. SIM Swap

Cybercriminals can call any mobile operator and pretend to be a credit card holder requesting a duplicate SIM card. In addition, they would ask the operator to deactivate the original cardholder's number. So, now the scammer can create new IDs, receive OTPs and execute online transactions.

If you ever receive a warning regarding a duplicate sim request or feel your number has been blocked. Immediately inform your mobile service operator and report about this. If you remain cautious and let the service provider know at the time, you will be able to prevent such scams.

6. Application Fraud

When identity theft happens, someone tries to impersonate you by using stolen documents to get a credit card under your name. If any criminal successfully completes this task, he will have a valid card to perform all kinds of monetary scams.

To avoid this kind of situation, you must keep track of whenever your IDs and other documents are used. In addition, if you have multiple copies of the same document and want to discard them, shred them before dumping them.

7. Hacking

One of the most common types of credit card fraud in India must be hacking. It is probably the oldest method of performing fraudulent activities. With the advancement of technology, hackers are also developing their skills. They can hack any of your devices and steal all your personal information.

Similarly, hackers can steal data from those firms with whom you have performed transactions. Thus, they can breach data for scams.

Although it is unpredictable to notice when you are hacked, so you need to be very careful while performing online transactions.

If any website seems suspicious, do not provide your details.

You also must not click on every link you get. These hackers can break into your online space and get the required data for conducting scams.

Scammers can use you card to buy money orders, gift cards, jewelry, send money via western union and have somebody with a fake I.D retrieve the funds.

Another common scam is when they order phones

offline from AT&T, Verizon, Sprint etc. When a scammer goes online to order phones, they're going to need a profile and your card info. Once on the website a scammer will choose 5 brand new iPhones or Galaxy's, and proceed to checkout the purchase.

At the check out window they will have the option to either pay the phones entire cost amount which will be well over $6K, or they can chose the financing option. Scammers usually chose the financing option, after selecting that option they will type in your name, social, DOB, address, any fake email they've created and wait for the website to do a credit check. Once the credit has been approved, the scammer only have to pay for the activation fee which is usually under $100 depending how high the victims credit score is. So that's 5 iPhones worth over $6,000 for less then $100. Scammers will use the victim real address for the billing and change the shipping address to an abandoned house address, or any address they have control over. Now imagine using that same information to get 5more phones from Verizon, then sprint.

That is a total of 15 phones, which can easily be sold for $900-$1,000 brand new in the box. That's a $13,500-$15,000 come up easy, all scammers have cash out man who buys anything they have to sell in bulk at a beneficial percentage.

The scam don't end here, usually when merchandise is shipped to a building a signature is needed upon delivery. Scammers wised up to this loop hole and have everything sent to home address, because the package can be left on your front step on delivery without a signature.

Scammers usually call and file a lost/stolen package claim, and get a whole new order of 15 phones all newly purchased phones they buy have warranty and insurance for that purpose.

CHAPTER SEVEN

CHECKS 1 ON 1

Check fraud is incredibly widespread. In fact, because there are so many different types of check fraud, no one has the exact numbers on how many people are affected or how much money is lost each year.

However, a 2016 global fraud study indicates that the typical organization loses 5% of its revenue every year due to fraud. The biggest culprit in these losses is asset misappropriation, and in that category, check tampering and billing schemes accounted for the biggest threats. Banks and other financial institutions face a heightened risk of these losses, and you need tools in place to protect yourself.

DEFINING CHECK FRAUD

Check fraud refers to any efforts to obtain money illegally using paper or digital checks.

This can include someone writing a bad check on their own account, forging a check in someone else's name, or drafting a completely fake check. But it can also include countless other types of fraud using checks.

THE HISTORY OF FRAUDULENT CHECKS

Although they have changed a lot over the years, checks in some form or another have existed since ancient times, and as trade spread from the Middle East into Europe in the middle ages and even more through the colonial era, checks became increasingly popular because they offered a convenient way to carry large sums of money. In contrast, bags of coins were cumbersome and subjected merchants to the risk of theft. However, fraud always plagued checks, and modern checks were developed around the idea of trying to thwart fraud.

IDENTIFYING TYPES OF CHECK FRAUD

Check fraud may be committed by your customers, or it may be perpetrated on your customers by thieves or scammers. Here are examples of some of the most common types of fraud:

* **Paperhanging** — When account holders purposefully write bad checks on their accounts.

* **Check Kiting** — When an account holder writes bad checks from their own account and deposits them in another account to create the illusion of a balance of the second account.

* **Check Floating** — When an account holder writes a check to another person or an individual, often in an attempt to buy a little time before they deposit funds into their account.

* **Check Forgery** — When someone forges an account holder's signature on a check.

* **Check Theft** — When someone steals someone else's paper check. Then, they use it to pay for goods or services, they deposit it in their own

account, or they try to cash it over the counter at your bank.

*Identity Check Theft — When someone opens an account in someone else's name and writes checks from it.

*Chemical Alteration — When a thief uses chemicals to erase the ink on a check so they can write something else. For instance, a thief might steal a check from a mailbox, erase the name of the intended recipient, write their own name, and cash the check. Alternatively, a scam artist may change the amount on a check using chemical alteration.

*Counterfeiting — When a scam artist steals someone's checking account information and prints a bunch of checks to use on their account.

*Money Order Fraud — With money order fraud, the scam artist convinces the victim to give them a check in exchange for a money order, but when the victim deposits the money order into their account, they discover that it's fake.

This is just the beginning. Thieves are always working on new ways to use checks in fraudulent ways.

FLOATING CHECKS FLIRT WITH DANGER

Unfortunately, many banking customers see floating checks as an innocuous activity. Often, they don't think much of writing a check a day or two before their paycheck or other deposit hits their account, but contrary to some beliefs, check floating can be very dangerous for financial institutions. In some cases, scam artists use the float time to engineer extensive scams that can lead to significant losses for financial institutions and their customers.

THE ECONOMIC IMPACT OF COUNTERFEIT CHECKS

Every year, scam artists draft millions of counterfeit checks worth billions of dollars, and financial institutions, merchants, and banking customers all face costs associated with counterfeit checks and other types of check fraud.

To protect your financial institution, you need to understand popular check scams and have tools in place to identify counterfeit checks.

CASHIER'S CHECKS AND MONEY ORDER SCAMS

Sometimes, rather than using checks, scam artists use cashier's checks or money orders to steal money from banks or victims. Although these scams take a variety of different forms, they often focus on convincing the victim to accept a large cashier's check in exchange for giving the thief some cash. Once the victim realizes the cashier's check is a fake, the scam artist is long gone with the victim's money.

PENALTIES FOR CHECK FRAUD

When people commit check fraud, they can face a range of penalties from fines to jail time to paying restitution to their victims. Typically, as the checks become larger or the assets obtained become more significant, the penalties become more severe. In most cases, check fraud is a state crime, but in some cases, check fraud can fall under federal jurisdiction.

HOW TO DETECT CHECK FRAUD

Ideally, you should have tools and processes in place that help you detect check fraud before it gets out of control. Bank tellers should know how to visually assess a check for signs of fraud, but you should also invest in machine learning software that can identify fraud flags based on the look of the check, its signature, and various other factors while also taking into account the customer's usual spending habits and looking for aberrations.

COUNTERFEIT CHECKS EXPLAINED

Counterfeit checks look like they are from bonafide bank accounts, but generally, they are not tied to any accounts. When a financial institution presents these checks for processing, they find out they are not real and cannot be cashed, but by that time, the scam artists are usually long gone. In many cases, account holders withdraw funds against these checks before realizing the checks are no good, and if the account holders don't have enough money to bring their accounts back into the black, the financial institutions may bear the losses.

HOW TO TELL IF A CHECK HAS BEEN ALTERED

Altered checks is another manifestation of check fraud. Scam artists may steal checks and alter a range of details from the static information on the check to the details written by the account holder. To protect your financial institution from losses associated from altered checks, you need well trained employees as well as tools that can look for minute alterations that may not be visible to the naked eye.

PROTECTING YOUR CLIENTS FROM CHECK FRAUD

To avoid check fraud, you need to educate your customers about the risks. Let them know that they need to be as careful with their digital information as they are with their paper information. For instance, they should always shred old checks before throwing them away, but they should also avoid doing electronic banking on public Wi-Fi and should change their passwords regularly.

Your business clients often face a larger risk of check fraud than your individual clients. In addition to taking the above steps, they should also use automatic bank reconciliation tools so they can spot anomalies right away, and they should know how to avoid phishing scams.

PREVENTING CHECK FRAUD

Perhaps, more importantly, your financial institution also needs tools in place to help you spot fraudulent checks. Ideally, you need software that can automatically inspect on-us checks and look for aberrations that suggest forgeries. Then, if the signature doesn't match, the font is off, the number out of order, or the information suspicious in any other way, the software flags the check for manual review. At that point, your staff can step in and verify whether the check is real. You may also want to integrate tools such as SENTRY: Seal. This essentially puts a seal or a unique barcode on every check. That code holds all the check's vital information, and if anything doesn't match, your system immediately finds the error.

It can be a brain teaser trying to figure out how fraudulent checks are made, scammers use real check software with stolen account/routing numbers. These information don't always have to be stolen, a scammer might know someone whose been in a car accident and the insurance company gave them a check.

All financial institution change their account number and routing number quarterly which is every 3months to prevent fraud, once a scammer get their hands on a check like that it's open season because nobody has more money than insurance companies. They can continue manipulating the check numbers, then mobile drop the check into a bank account and take that same physical check to a check cashing location and cash it again.

Usually, it takes about two business days for a check to clear. That can vary from check to check, though. Banks may withhold check deposits for several days to ensure that the funds are available and the check doesn't bounce before you spend that money.

If you spend the funds and then the check bounces, you could incur a fee.

There are a few factors that might cause a check to clear faster than two days. Banks are generally required by law to make the first $225 of a check deposit available by the next business day. For example, if the check is deposited on a weekend, it's considered to be deposited on Monday, so the first $225 of the check will be available on Tuesday.

The $225 rule does not apply to accounts within the first 30 days of opening, however. Some checks are designed to clear faster than a standard check, and these will become available in full by the next business day.

These checks include:

Checks issued by the governmentCertified checks Cashier's checks Checks from the same financial institutionDepositing a check at a bank

Depositing a check at a bank or credit union branch is often the quickest way to have access tothose funds.

As long as the check is deposited before the institution's specified cut-off time, it should be available within a day or two. While the cut-off time for a branch deposit can vary, it can't be earlier than 2 p.m., by law.

Mobile check deposit

Mobile check deposit, which allows you to deposit a check by taking photos of it through your bank's mobile app, typically takes the same amount of time as an in-person deposit, though it may take a bit longer to process in some cases.

Mobile check deposits come with cut-off times, too. At Bank of America, for example, a mobile check must be deposited by 9 p.m. ET (for Eastern and

Central time zones) or 8 p.m. PT (for Mountain and Pacific time zones) for it to clear by the next business day.If a check is taking longer to clear than your bank's typical processing time, it's probably because the bank placed an extended hold on it.

The bank will likely notify you of any holds on the deposit receipt (if the check is deposited at a branch) or the deposit confirmation screen (if the check is deposited through an app). The institution may also notify you by text notification, email or mail if a hold comes up after the time of deposit.

Some reasons a financial institution may extend a check's hold include:

There's reasonable cause to believe the funds are uncollectible (such as suspected fraud).

The check has been redeposited.

The check amount exceeds $5,525. (Note: Only the amount that's over $5,525 can be held for longer.)

The receiving account is new or has been repeatedly overdrawn. The check is from an international bank.

In these cases, the financial institution may hold the check for up to a week, after which the funds will clear or the check will bounce.

Next up is understand the check float system. In financial terms, the float is money within the banking system that is briefly counted twice due to time gaps in registering a deposit or withdrawal.

These time gaps are usually due to the delay in processing paper checks.

A bank credits a customer's account as soon as a check is deposited. However, it takes some time to receive a check from the payer's bank and record it. Until the check clears the account it is drawn on, the amount it is written for "exists" in two different places, appearing in the accounts of both the recipient's and payer's banks.

KEY TAKEAWAYS

The float is essentially double-counted money: a paid sum which, due to delays in processing,

appears simultaneously in the accounts of the payer and the payee.

Individuals and companies alike can use float to their advantage, gaining time or earning interest before payment clears their bank.

Playing with float can spill into the realm of wire fraud or mail fraud if it involves the use of others' funds.

The Federal Reserve (The Fed) defines two types of float. Holdover float results from delays at the processing institution, typically due to the weekend and seasonal backlogs. Transportation float occurs due to inclement weather and air traffic delays and is, therefore, highest in the winter months.

The Fed—which processes one-third of all checks in the United States—observes that although the amount of float fluctuates randomly, there are definite weekly and seasonal trends. For example, float usually increases on a Tuesday due to a backlog of checks over the weekend and during the months of December and January because of higher check volume during the holiday season.

The Federal Reserve uses these trends to forecast float levels, which are then used in the actual day-to-day implementation of monetary policy.1

How to Calculate Float

The formula to calculate float is: Float = firm's available balance – firm's book balance

The float represents the net effect of checks in the process of clearing. A common measure of a float is the average daily float, calculated by dividing the total value of checks in the collection process during a specified period by the number of days in the period. The total value of checks in the collection process is calculated by multiplying the amount of float by the number of days it is outstanding.

For example, a company with $15,000 of float outstanding for the first 14 days of the month, and $19,000 for the last 17 days of the month will calculate its average daily float as:

[($15,000 x 14) + ($19,000 x 17)] ÷ 31

$$= (\$210{,}000 + \$323{,}000) \div 31$$

$$= \$533{,}000 \div 31$$

$$= \$17{,}193.55$$

The Uses of Float

Individuals often use float to their advantage. For example, Amanda has a credit card payment for $500 due April 1. On March 23, she writes and mails a check-in that amount, even though she doesn't have $500 in her bank account. However, she knows that her paycheck will be deposited in her checking account by March 25—and she counts on the fact that the credit card company probably won't receive and present her check for payment until April 1. She has $500 worth of float—the time between the writing of her check and the time her check clears—for those days.

If she were tech-savvy, she could essentially do the same thing by going online on March 23 and scheduling an electronic payment on the credit card company's website for April 1, again counting for her bank to have posted her paycheck by March 25.

The Future of Float

Technological advances have spurred the adoption of measures that substantially speed up payment and hence reduce float. These measures include the widespread use of electronic payments and electronic funds transfers, the direct deposit of employee paychecks by companies, and the scanning and electronic presentation of checks—instead of their physical transfer.

As a result, float in the United States declined from a record daily average of $6.6 billion in the late 1970s—when it spiked due to high inflation and high-interest rates—to only $774 million in 2000, according to the Federal Reserve.1

The steady decline in the number of checks written each year, combined with the rapid adoption of innovative and convenient payment services, may make float a thing of the past.

Real World Example of Float

Large companies and financial institutions also often "play the float" with larger sums for-profit—namely, the interest income they earn on an amount by speeding up its deposit into their accounts or slowing down a presentation for payment. Such moves are not illegal, either for individuals or for institutions, if the money involved is all their own. However, playing with float can spill into the realm of wire fraud or mail fraud if it involves the use of others' funds.

In 1985, the brokerage firm E.F. Hutton & Company (now defunct) pleaded guilty to 2,000 charges for deliberately and systematically overdrawing some accounts to fund other accounts. The firm was writing checks on money it did not have to profit from the float—in effect, getting millions in loans from the banks without the banks' knowledge and without paying fees or interest. It was, in essence, a floating scheme, executed on a grandiose scale for years.

Since the float is essentially double-counted money, it can distort the measurement of a nation's money supply by briefly inflating the amount of money in the banking system.

A popular way float time is used is by doing check kiting. The traditional method of check kiting is called circular kiting, and it has been around for a long time. However, as the financial system has grown more complex, check kiting has given birth to different subvariants. Here are some of the most common check kiting schemes.

Circular kiting is the simplest form of check kiting. For example, say you work with two different banks and have multiple accounts at each bank. You write a check from Bank A for $500.

However, you only have $10 in your checking account at Bank A. You go to Bank B and deposit this check for $500.

You then go back the next day and withdraw the $500 in cash from Bank B before your original check from Bank A has time to clear or bounce.

By then, you only had $10 but just withdrew $500. That same day, you write a check to Bank A to cover the amount of the $500 check you wrote for Bank B. So this cycle will continue until you get caught.

In a more advanced form of kiting, you would not only involve you and yourself but different people as well. You continuously write bad checks to each other, seeing how long you can take advantage of withdrawing hard cash during the float time.

Check kiting usually involves business owners, since it's usual for business owners to do big transactions through their accounts, imagine them doing everything stated above except instead of $500 - they're writing $100,000 - $1million dollar checks at a time without having to worry about the bank red flagging them on the first couple transaction

CHAPTER EIGHT

Versa Check

The Write Checks screen allows you to write checks drawn off of any bank or money market account that you setup with an electronic checkbook in Versa Check. Using the pull down menu under the Write Checks header will allow you to choose from which account to draw the checks.

The Account button allows you access to the following account functions:

- New Account: opens the New Account dialog box
- Edit Account: opens the Edit Account dialog box
- Edit Checkbook: opens the Checkbook Setup for accounts which use a checkbook
- Reconcile: opens the Reconcile wizard which allows you to reconcile an account from bank

statements or other records

The New Check icon will clear the current check on screen once you have finished a check, and allow you to write additional checks.

1. Choose if the check should be printed or sent in the Number pull down menu.

2. Correct the Date of the check if using a date other than the current day's date.

3. Enter the total of the check in the Amount field.

4. Use the pull down menu or type in a new name for the payee.

5. Use the Memo field for whatever memo you wish to have printed on the check.

6. The Reference field may be used to add personal reference information if you wish.

7. The pull down menu for Category* can be used to assign a category for the check payment, for

example "Job Expense" or "Health care."By using the Split button, you may itemize a check payment.

8. If funding for the check must be approved, click the 'Approval required' check box. Click here for detailed instructions for check approvals.

Checks to be printed will be added to the list of checks under the To Print tab found underneath the check form. You may use the Sort filter to list checks according to date, number, payee, etc

CHAPTER NINE:

TPICAL FRAUD SITE

5 dumps+pin platinium=300$

10 dumps+pin visa and Master Card=250$ 20 dumps+pin classic=150$ wrong with the dump we will replace it with no questions. Minimum Order

5pcs=$100 50pcs=$750

More than 100pcs=$10/1

CVV Fullz USA.

MSR606------$180

EMBOSSER---$150

ATM SKIMMER WINCOR $330

NCR-------$300

LIBERTY RESERVE HACK $150

CVV2 AND Bank logins

I Seller Cvv2 (US,UK,AU,Italia,EURO, and dob+sn+full info and bank login TANGERINE SUNTRUST

CITIBANK SOUTH DAKOTA, N.A

LLOYDS TSB BA

Fresh Cards. Selling Dumps, Cvvs, Fullz.

Hello. We selling fresh dumps with original Track1 and Track

There are normal cc`s with cvv code,USA fullz,UK+DOB.All stuff is checked and approved.

ONLY ORIGINAL INFO!

We have approved fresh dumps from USA, large bases.Visa Classic, MC Standart - $15

Visa Gold, Platinum, Business, Signature - $25. IF YOU ORDER OVER 20 pcs:

Visa Classic, MC Standart - $8/1 Visa Gold, Platinum, Business, Signature - $20/1 We have EU dumps also. Visa Classic, MC Standart - $50/1 Visa Gold, Platinum,

Business, Signature - $130/1 Formate is:

5401683030957507=09091012000024

;

B5401683030957507^DAVIES/TOKUB

O ^09091012000000294000000

Prices for normal CC is so: USA - $7.

UK - $12. Formate is:

Card Number | Exp. Date | CVV/CVV2 | First Name |
Last Name | Street | City | State | Zip Code | Country |
Phone | Type Of Card | Bank Name |

If you r interested in Fullz:

USA - $25.

UK(cvv+dob) - $30

We sell information only good quality, We don't offer bull**** stuff. Less price have rippers only. Be patient ih have any delays. We do all so fast how we can. we thank for your understanding.

Service takes care of valid only, not their balance.

It's available to sort cvvs by Classic/Gold/Platinum types, not giving any warranty of high amount balance. Service can deny to process Ur requerst witout explanation of reasons. I SELL LOGINS AND CVV,s

1 Visa card   3$

1 US card....................7$

1 CA card ....12$

1 EU card ....12$

1 AU card ....18$

1 JP Card ....18$

1 Track 1& 2 CC............................20$

1 Fresh Fullz ....25$

1 Dead Fullz...............................10$

1 Paypal verified without balance==50$

1 Paypal verified with 1000$ balance ==100$

BALANCE   IN   CHASE   70K   TO   155K ========200$

BALANCE IN WASHOVIA ....24K   TO 80K===========100$

BALANCE IN BOA ....75K   TO 450K==========350$

BALANCE IN CREDIT UNION ....ANY

AMOUNT=========250$

BALANCE IN HALIFAX..............ANY

AMOUNT=========250$

BALANCE IN COMPASS ....ANY

AMOUNT=========400$

BALANCE IN WELSFARGO........ANY

AMOUNT=========250$

YOU CAN CONTACT FOR MANY MORE OTHER BANK LOG YOU NEED...

1. COMERSUS SOFTWARE WITH BANK LOG IN AND BANK CREDIT CARD CODE

   ==========2000$

2. COMERSUS SOFTWARE WITHOUT BANK LOG IN AND BANK CREDIT CARD CODE ==========1500$

3. NEW WESTERN UNION HACKING BUG FOR WORLD WIDE TRANSFER

   ===================500

4. NEW PAYPAL LOG IN HACKWARE FOR HACKING   FRESH   PAYPAL

=======================650$

5. NEW SHOP ADMIN HACKWARE FOR HACKING ONLINE SHOP FOR CREDIT CARD============2000$

6. NEW CREDIT CARD AMOUNT CHECKER FOR PEOPLE WANTING TO KNOW AMOUNT ON CC===320$

7. NEW CREDIT CARD VALIDATOR FOR VALIDATING ANY FULL CC INFO

====================320$

....

. ...…

.>24 hours for Hold-Call / Pick Up Card:

04 | Hold-Call Or Pick Up Card

07 | Hold-Call Or Pick up Card | Pick Up Card - Special Condition

41 | Hold-Call Or Pick up Card | Pick Up Card - Lost

43 | Hold-Call Or Pick up Card | Pick Up Card Stolen

Please read it carefully:

1. We don't send binlist so ask for it

2. Don't ask for free test. We don't give free Test

3. We sell information only good quality, We don't offer bull**** stuff. Less price have rippers only.

If you can't trust our service, we have good reviews in this post or ask us for forum's list where we have been registered.

Cvv MA$TERS TEAM IS HERE FRESH LIVE================

US visa/US master $2.5 Random with Bin $1 extra fee US amex/US discover $3.5 Random

US FULLINFO CC $25 DOB SSN MMN only Randon with Bin $5 extra fee MIX CC ONLY

UK CC NORMAL $9 WITH DOB $19 Randon with Bin $1 extra fee EU Visa / Master / Amex $10

AU Visa / Master $7

AU amex $10

CANADA cc $10 ITALY cc $11

ASIA cc $17

We offer 100% Worldwide fresh US,UK EU CCV/DUMP and fullinfo ccs DEMO:

Austria

Linda Csencsits| Johann Sebastian Bach Gasse 7 |
Eisenstadt | Austria

| AT | A-7000 | Linda

Csencsits |0043/69912820952 | l.c...@gmx.net | Card |
MC | 5449672710182012 |891/5 |2011 | Pass VBV.
France 456107900068111104 | 10 | 400 | Benjamin
chayette | 9 rue benjamin godard | 75116 | | paris | FR |
Pass VBV. Germany 1096 | Dr. Jan Hagen |
4779127000301491 | 0211 | 056 | Jan Hagen |
Breitestr. 1 | Berlin | 10178 | | Deutschland | 030
21231 8030 | ha...@esmt.org Pass VBV. Spain
97261/MONTE
GANETA5?C/BILBAO/48014/NULL/626677175/BAR
BARA/REGALADO//5540610501623567/12/2011/2
53/BARBARA
REGALADOVALENZUELA/mc/ES/ Pass VBV.
Turkey93239/EskisehirOsmangaziUniversity/Eskisehir/
26030/NULL/(90) 532 5283075/Mujgan/Sagir/
\5437712233074303/06/2011/352/MujganSagir/mc/TR/
Pass VBV. Poland 92834/Dolna 7/Warsaw/00

773/NULL/8-903-5200   244/Arkadiusz/Sugier/

/4289150060282800/04/2012/365/Arkadiusz

Sugier/visa/PL/ Pass VBV. Switzerland 95158/108 111,Raheja   Chambers,Free P/Mumbai/4000021/NULL/9820428794/   Mr Puneet/Makar/ /4629860006399000/12/2011/297/Mr Puneet Makar/visa/IN/ Pass VBV. Czech Repulic 98249/Wannenstrasse 44/Uster/8610/NULL/+41 43 3174520/Marianne/ Arvidsson//375895478452006/09/2011/3824/Marianne Arvidsson/amex/CH/ Pass VBV.

Mexico |martha yolanda montero cruz |4931720010392438|02|2012|869|Visa| MIGUEL| GOMEZ||calle laja# 20 sm 523|fracc. la piedra|cancun quintana roo|NA|77506| 9989149404| MX | Pass VBV.

===

1 TIME CVV FREE LIVE DEMO NEW BUYERS ONLY!!!

We GIVE 1 CC Random FOR FREE OR TEST 1 TIME ONLY NEW CUSTOMER...THERE ARE NO MIN ORDER..YOU ARE WELCOME TO BUY 1 OR 2 TO TEST! PAYMENT VIA WU/MG LR WMZ UKASH ONLY OR TRADE..

WHEN YOU READY TO BUY JUST PM US ON YAHOO msg YM: cvvmast...@ymail.com or ICQ 554914762

Regards, CvvMASTERS Team Peace </pre> </HTML> Wholesale dealer VERIFIE CVV SELLER (Uk,Eu Asia with bulk), VERIFIED DUMPS SELLER or Dumps with Pin, Hosting Cpanel.

Mailers(Inbox Mailer,Webmail Mailers),SMTP INBOX ANY E_MAIL INBOX Sent, Track 1&2. Sell cvv:usa-uk-eu-jp-ger-euro-ita-ca-au-asia-fra-sweden-findland- poland-belgium-inreland-New caledonia-Slovenoa-Denmark-Taiwan-Swiizerland with dob + ssn all country good and fresh very cheap here banks login:us-uk-eu+ paypal+dumps track123+pin+wu transfer! contact me if u need..

New cvv For Sale With low Price Fullz 7$ US,UK,Europe,Jp,SW paypal with balance+ email access im selling cc,fullz,dumps,bank login,paypal,wu trf,paypalbin im sellingcc,fullz,dumps,bank login,paypal,wu trf,paypalbin russia

I'm Seller for: CC, CVV US,UK,CA, EURO,AU, Italian,Japan,France, all cc. Paypal verify, Software Spam mail + mail list, code PHP,Shop Admin and CC fullz info, CC DOB, Dump, Banklogin, Pri sockDomain hosting cc/enroll/dump+pin Western Union Transfers Online® and selling Account Paypal Login with 2K Balance Verify Paypal Money Hack 2011 / (Updated of Wu Bug [V]ersion 2.0.1.0) Who's neez BUZZ me now?Sell cvv (Uk,Eu with bulk), I SELL, RANDOM LEADS,MAILER,SMTP,WEBMAIL

CVV,FULLZ,BANK LOGINS,DUMPS+PINS, TRACK 1&

2. dumps or dumps with pin. Track1&Track2, Mailers(inbox mailer, Webmail Mailer Hosting

Cpanel. Selling Fresh Live CC All Country,Dumps CC,Trac1,Track 2,Bank login,CCadmin,Admin Login,Mailer,Smtp,SQL injection,fresh Sock/Proxy and many more , Now Available For Sale RDP, SMTP, SSH, FTP, VPN, VNC, LEADS, SOcks, Http/Https proxy, Socks 4&5 , Sock Admin, CC, Paypal, Fresh Email+pass Usa, Usa Number, Personalised Domain, Mailers +customised, cPanel, Webftp buzz me now For Deals!!! Buzz me if u need any stuff ,I am good to my buyer.. poker game vegas casino gambling euro bets blackjack Blizzard starcraft2 beta cdkey cd-key patch fix exploit all version reload hacker lab hacking hackers nmap sectools.org indishell.in hackerz2live packet sniffer magstripe data on the credit and debit cards payoneer prepaid defCon 2006 hackers ATM withdrawals E-Gold and Web Money magstripe data onto counterfeit credit cards fraudulent webmoney withdrawals carders Carder.cc carderz CallService.bizcardersmarket.com dumpsforum.comBSell credit card information, credit card debit card, 101.201, stolen credit cards, cloned credit cards, counterfeit credit cards, credit card fraud; La vente de carte de crédit, carte de crédit, carte de débit, 101.201, les cartes de crédit volées, cloné des cartes de crédit, la contrefa?on de cartes de crédit, les fraudes par carte de crédit; hack, hacking, hacker, psc hack hack, brute force, bruter, paysafecard hacking, hacked, elite, 1337, crew, r@p1dshar3, h@ck3r, l33t, leet, 101,201, La venta de información de tarjeta de crédito, tarjeta de crédito tarjeta de débito, 101,201, tarjetas de crédito robadas, clonadas las tarjetas de crédito, la falsificación de tarjetas de crédito, fraude de tarjetas de crédito; ?????,??????? 101.201 cardersunion.net dump fullz, skimmer for sale, fakepassport sale, skimmer supplier, cardingworld forum, fake driver license,cashout drops, plastic holograms, carder fraud forum, selling dumps,cashout dumps, atm fraud, infraud.su infraud.ws , cvv hacker forum, money mule, 1337crew forum , netcarding , fakacarda , cardersunion , cardingempire ,lava- carding , cardingworld , cardersmarket , ccpower , underground seller, mybazaar , kurupt forum , 1337 crew forum ,

offcarding , carders.eu ,offcarding forum , fraud money laundering Sell cvv2:USA-UK-EU-JP-GER-EUROPE-INTER-SWEDEN-CA-AU-FRANCE

INDIANEW UPDATES= ITALY-ISRAEL,JORDAN,KAZAKHSTAN,KOREA REPUBLIC,LEBANON,MALAYSIA,PERU,PUER O RICO,SLOVAKIA, SOUTH AFRICA,SWITZERLAND, TURKEY,UAE,USA,UK,VENEZUELA,ANDORA,B AHRAIN,BULGARIA,ANDORRA,AUSTRIA,HUNG ARY S,EGYOT,DOMINICAN,CHINA ,JAPAN, CANADA Sell Cvv Hongkong +Singapore+Korea+Japan+France +Germany +UK Dob + Newzeland +Netherland+Belgium+Srilanka+Malaysia+Norway+ Spain+Turkey+Taiwan +Afganistan With Dob and SSn

i have some cc AU, UK, RU, Chile, IRELAND, NEW

ZEALAND for sell now. who need pls contact me now!

I have EU now Belgium Poland Denmark Finland Ireland Turkey Portugal Bulgaria Croatia With dob +ssn FRESH SAUDI ARABIA, UAE, JAPAN SINGAPORE, CHINA, CCV UK, USA GERMANY DOB, FRANCE NON DOB , AUSTRALIA, CANADA, SPAIN CCV, NETHERLAND CCV, EMAIL LEADS EMAIL PASS LISTS, SMTPS, FRESH FRESH FRESH magstripe data magstripe data crack the PINs decryption of PIN

CHAPTER TEN

FRAUD PROTECTION

Honestly there's no such thing as privacy or fraud prevention. The only way to prevent fraud is to go off the grid and erase your existence, which means never using your name, social, or credit cards anywhere. Sounds harsh and impossible right? I know it is.

Again this is why I wrote this book, because I realized there's no way you can truly stop fraud, there's too many ways to manipulate the system and technology. And as the saying goes a sucker is born every minute on planet earth, but once your competent to the common tricks and tactics you will be more secure.

Knowledge is key to everything. You not knowing about fraud will get you scammed everytime, but now that your eyes are open watch how alert you will be during every transaction.

Always watch who you give your credit/debit card too, make sure they don't leave your sight with it or swipe it through any black boxes.
Burn all your mail before throwing them away, and inspect all gas stations, ATMs, and store POS machines before you insert your card and pi